HIKING

from A to Z

by

John McKinney

www.TheTrailmaster.com

Hiking from A to Z By John McKinney
Hiking from A to Z © 2012 The Trailmaster, Inc. All
rights reserved. Manufactured in the United States of
America by MiniBük. No part of this book may be used
or reproduced in any manner whatsoever without written
permission except in the case of brief quotations embod-
ied in articles and reviews.

ISBN: 978-0-934161-42-8
Cover and interior design by Christian Ophus
Layout and e-book by Lisa DeSpain
HIKE Series Editor: Cheri Rae

Published by Olympus Press and The Trailmaster, Inc.
www.TheTrailmaster.com (Visit our site for a complete
listing of all Trailmaster publications, products, and
services)

Although The Trailmaster, Inc. and the author have made every
attempt to ensure that information in this book is accurate, they
are not responsible for any loss, damage, injury, or inconvenience
that may occur to you while using this information. You are responsible for your own safety; the fact that an activity or trail is
described in this book does not mean it will be safe for you. Trail
conditions can change from day to day; always check local conditions and know your limitations.

INTRODUCTION

THE IDEA for a hiker's dictionary came to me a few years ago when I was speaking to the annual California Recreational Trails Conference, a gathering of the state's top trail-builders and advocates. One of the points of my talk was that we trail enthusiasts have a jargon of our own. If we want to communicate effectively with each other—and the general public—we need to define our terms.

We all had a long laugh when I read a mock press release about the grand opening of a new trail that was chock full of incomprehensible-to-the-layperson language about stakeholders and staging areas, VDs (Visitor Days), and viewsheds.

Ridiculous?

Of course. But it occurred to me that as a "hiking writer" I had for the past thirty years used a vocabulary that was particular to hikers and likely peculiar to non-hikers, but had never been defined.

"If you wish to converse with me, define your terms," declared Voltaire, the great French writer and philosopher. And as a cautionary note to those blazing new trails, Voltaire also wryly observed: "Our wretched species is so made that those who walk on the well-trodden path always throw stones at those who are showing a new road."

My academic training prepared me to talk about hiking on radio and TV and make videos; I had no further higher education except for lessons learned while hiking up mountains. I've written a few dozen books and a thousand articles about hiking and nature; not a single one of them is footnoted.

My work in the field of hiking has been, quite literally, in the field. It's my hope that this considerable field research will add to the hiker's fun and knowledge of hiking. So take a hike.

And then look up "take a hike" in this dictionary.

Hike on.

John McKinney

About this Book

Hiking from A to Z, with its definitions of hiking words and terms, can be loosely defined as a dictionary: "a reference book containing an alphabetical list of words with information about them."

Traditionalists and your high school English teacher would likely frown at this definition, regarding it as too simplistic, insisting that a true dictionary must include more than definitions. Not surprisingly, that august authority, Webster's Dictionary, defines dictionary in a more expansive way as "a collection of words . . . often listed alphabetically, with usage information, definitions, phonetics, pronunciations and other information."

Hiking from A to Z could be considered a glossary: "A list of often difficult or specialized words with their definitions, often placed at the back of a book." Like an ill-fitting backpack on a hiker, a glossary gets us on the trail but is not really suited to go very far very fast. Some of the hiking-related words are specialized (and therefore appropriate for a glossary), but many are not. Very few hiking words and terms are difficult to pronounce or to understand.

I suppose *Hiking from A to Z* could be considered a lexicon, defined as: "A stock of terms used in a particular profession, subject, or style." However the chief—and virtually only—synonym for lexicon is dictionary, so I saw no purpose in substituting an uncommon word for a common one.

Besides, we habitually look up words in a dictionary (often an online one these days), not in a glossary or a lexicon.

So dictionary it is. Expect definitions of hiker-specific words, and more common words, defined from a hiker's point of view. Don't expect the breakdown of a word into syllables, however, or an account of a word's origin from Greek-Latin-French or whatever roots.

Only a few dozen of the words and terms in this dictionary can be considered "Hiker only." The Trailmaster's heavy editorial hand is most evident in the definitions of "hiker" words.

I've long been an advocate for hiking and for hiking trails and the compilation of this dictionary is very much a part of that. I make no apology for my hiker-centric point of view. I appreciate other forms of outdoor recreation, but will leave it to others to create lexicons for cyclists, equestrians, and canoeists.

Many words point to the intersection and over-lap of hiking with the life sciences, earth sciences, government, as well as other forms of outdoor recreation. Like many hikers I know, I have a strong pro-nature streak, and this publication reflects the desire to share my natural history interest from the hiker's point of view.

Since I am a West Coast resident, I have a certain sensitivity to what I perceive as the biases of other national hiking publications and feel compelled to counter them in this volume. Most definitions of hiking words and the hiking experience are eastern-centric; that is to say they reflect the point of view of hikers in the eastern United States. For example, brooks and streams are carefully defined but often there is no mention of creeks and arroyos, terms used in the western United States.

While proudly nationalistic, U.S. hikers need to embrace the other hikers in North America and the considerable and ever-increasing numbers of hikers, English-speaking and not, who visit here. "Think globally, hike locally," I say. I've sprinkled in some foreign words in the dictionary and added very brief samplings of hiker words in Spanish, French, Italian, and, for lack of a better term, "English English," words and terms from England, Ireland, and Scotland. (See "English English for Hikers" at the end of the dictionary definitions in this volume.)

Credit Where Credit is Due

This dictionary is a compilation of material from many other sources, from words and terms published in books over the last fifty years, including several hundred publications in my own library.

Many of the trail terms and definitions, particularly the more technical ones, used in this volume were first compiled for and published in *Trails Primer: A Glossary of Trails, Greenway, and Outdoor Recreation Terms and Acronyms* (2001, Jim Schmid, editor, South Carolina Department of Parks, Recreation and Tourism, Columbia, SC).

Schmid's heroic pioneering effort has been revised and updated by others in the trail-building community. The latest incarnation of Schmid's comprehensive work can be found online at AmericanTrails.org.

Trail terminology is only one component in *Hiking from A to Z*, which also taps many many references to define nature-oriented words and terms. My favorite of many geology-geography resources is Geology.com. For certain environmental words and terms, I appreciated definitions from the Natural Resources Defense Council (NRDC.org).

The Hiker Defined and Redefined

With so many who like to hike, it's surprising that the word "hiker" lacks a widely accepted popular definition. This lack of a clear definition—much less a rich and transformative one—presents both a challenge and an opportunity.

A challenge to overcome is the sometimes negative, sometimes nonsensical defining of a hiker by the popular media. It's enough to convince any would-be hiker or hesitant hiker to stay home.

The huge opportunity is to redefine and to refine the definition of a hiker, illuminate the many pleasures and satisfactions available to one who hikes and, in so doing, point out the benefits to the mind, body and spirit along the way.

If we who love to hike don't define what a hiker is, others (non-hikers to be sure) will do it for us. We've all seen hikers poorly portrayed in the media—as goofy gals and macho guys, as crazed survivalists and tender-footed nincompoops. Even worse are the TV news reports that sensationalize stories about lost, injured or dead hikers. Rarely do these reports get the facts straight and often those they characterize as "hikers" are anything but: a family that wanders away from the RV campground; motorists stranded on a road to nowhere who have to walk back to civilization; the ill-prepared storm-forecast ignoring urbanite whose only survival skill is dialing 911 on a cell phone that unfortunately has no reception in the wilderness; numbskulls who fail to heed warning signs and step over ledges or get stomped by bison.

The dictionary definition of a hiker is a simple one:

Hiker One who hikes (especially frequently); a foot traveler; someone who goes on an extended walk in the mountains or country (for pleasure)

There is nothing wrong with the dictionary definition of a hiker—as far as it goes.

It just doesn't go very far or very deep.

Surely hiking and being a hiker means more. One purpose of this book is to expand upon and refine the definition of a hiker by presenting the many aspects of what it is to explore the world afoot.

However, before moving on to an alternative or expanded view of the hiker, several words in the dictionary definition require closer examination. "Frequently" is frequently part of the definition, suggesting one must hike often in order to be a true hiker. I've known hikers who discuss—and a few who obsess about—the frequency of their hiking adventures. Most hikers wish we could state confidently, "I hike frequently" rather than say wistfully, "I wish I could get out more frequently."

Both those who hike and those who don't assume that there is an unofficial requirement that a person must take a certain number of hikes over a particular time period in order to be a hiker or to remain a hiker in good standing. One hike per week? One per month? Twenty, thirty or forty per year?

I'm certain that it's not a number at all. As if expressing little confidence that a hiker need hike "frequently" to be a hiker, dictionaries almost always put the word "frequently" in parentheses.

How often should a hiker hike?

"As often is possible" is one good answer. "Whenever and wherever you can," is another. It's definitely not a particular number of hikes taken in a particular time frame.

Another element of the dictionary definition of hiker that deserves scrutiny is "extended." A walk extended from what? A longer than normal walk? What would be a normal walk and what would be a prolonged one?

I can live with the dictionary definition of a hike being an extended walk, and I suspect most hikers can as well. I'm guessing that non-hikers and those disliking hiking would argue that the dictionary use a more pejorative term than extended, such as aimless, arduous, unnecessary, purposeless or hellish.

Ah, some people fear what they do not know and do not know what they're missing. I say remove the parenthesis from "for pleasure" in the definition of hiker. A hiker is one who hikes for pleasure not one who hikes (for pleasure). Let's not be tentative here.

Is it correct to define a hiker as one who walks? Absolutely. Everyone who speaks of hiking routinely uses the words walk and hike interchangeably. But there's an important difference to remember: Every hike is a walk, but not every walk is a hike. There are many ways to shade the differences between a walk and a hike, but the most essential difference is in locale: To go hiking is to go green.

A hiker walks "in the mountains or country" as the dictionary puts it. Hikers also walk along lakeshores, seashores, through forests and across prairies and in many other natural environments. The point is a hiker walks in the natural world or at least a reasonable facsimile, such as an undeveloped park or botanical garden.

Now go take a hike! And please contribute to the next edition of *Hiking from A to Z* with your favorite hiking words and definitions.

—The Trailmaster

Hiking from A to Z

Access The opportunity to approach, enter, or make use of public lands.

Access Points Designated areas and passageways that allow the public to reach a trail from adjacent streets or community facilities.

Access Trail Any trail that connects the main trail to a town, road, or another trail system.

Acclimatization The gradual process of becoming physiologically accustomed to high altitude.

Acre A measure of area equal to 43,560 square feet. One square mile equals 640 acres.

Acute Mountain Sickness (AMS) A condition characterized by shortness of breath, fatigue, headache, nausea, and other flu-like symptoms. It occurs at high altitude and is attributed to a shortage of oxygen. Most people don't experience symptoms until they reach heights well above 5,000 feet.

Adopt-A-Trail A program in which groups or businesses "adopt" trails, providing volunteer work parties at periodic intervals to help maintain the trail. Though no special trail privileges are granted, the trail manager generally acknowledges that a trail has been "adopted" by erecting signs that indicate the trail is part of an Adopt-A-Trail program and include the name of the adopter.

Aerobic An intensity of exercise that allows the body's need for oxygen to be continually met. This intensity can be sustained for long periods. Aesthetics Relates to the pleasurable characteristics of a physical environment as perceived through the five senses of sight, sound, smell, taste, and touch.

Alignment The layout of the trail in horizontal and vertical planes. The bends, curves, and ups and downs of the trail. The more the alignment varies, the more challenging the trail.

Alluvial Pertaining to material that is carried and deposited by running water.

Alluvial Fan A low, outspread, relatively flat to gently sloping mass of loose rock material deposited by a stream where it flows from a narrow mountain valley onto a plain or broad valley.

Alpine Of, or relating to, or characteristic of the Alps or their inhabitants. Of or relating to high mountains. Living or growing on mountains above the timberline—for example, alpine plants. Intended or concerned with mountaineering.

Alpine Start Predawn departure from camp in order to reach a summit before snowmelt becomes problematic.

Altimeter An instrument for measuring altitude.

Altitude The height of a thing or place measured Above Ground Level or from Mean Sea Level.

Amenities Any element used to enhance the user's experience and comfort along a trail.

Anaphylactic Shock An extreme allergic reaction in some people (caused by the body producing too much histamine) when stung by bees, wasps, yellow jackets, etc. Reactions include red skin, itchy hives, and the closing of the airways. If susceptible to anaphylaxis it would be wise to carry an Anakit prescribed by your doctor.

Ancient Forest A forest that is typically older than 200 years with large trees, dense canopies and an abundance of diverse wildlife.

Anorak Wind-proof jacket with hood attached. No front zipper.

Arête French term for a narrow or pointy spot on a ridge.

Arid A climate or region in which precipitation is

deficient in quantity or occurs infrequently

Arroyo A dry creek bed that fills with water after a heavy rain.

Artifacts Any object made, modified, or used by humans.

Ascent An upward slope or incline or process of rising or going upward.

Ascent, First A much-coveted prize; first to climb a certain peak or climbing route.

Axe (Ax) A tool with a long handle and bladed head (single bit—one sharp side or double bit—sharp sides) for chopping deadfall from trails.

Azimuth The degree of bearing from your current position to a landmark.

Backcountry An area where there are no maintained roads or permanent buildings—just primitive roads and trails.

Backpack (Backpacking) A large pack worn on the back to carry camping supplies. To go on an overnight hike carrying your supplies in a backpack.

Backpack, External Frame A backpack supported by an exposed frame.

Backpack, Internal Frame Concealed frame supports pack.

Bail (Bail Out) To halt (perhaps temporarily) one's planned or intended outdoor trip, often due to sickness, injury, exhaustion, or change in weather conditions.

Balaclava A form-fitting hood (fleece, wool, or synthetic) that covers not only the head but also the face and neck, it can be worn as a cap or pulled down over the ears to protect your face from wind.

Bald Mountain with an open, grassy summit that's void of trees.

Bandanna A square of cloth, usually cotton, with many more uses than just a scarf.

Bar A sand or gravel deposit in a streambed that is often exposed only during low water periods.

Barricade A portable or fixed barrier having object markings, used to close all or a portion of the trail right-of-way to traffic.

Base Camp A semi-permanent camp set up after traveling into an area from which day trips for trail work or enjoyment can be made. This allows hikers to leave heavy gear in one place for several days.

Base Layer The layer of clothing closest to the skin.

Baseline A line of reference crossing your path of travel used to make following a compass bearing closer to foolproof. Baselines include roads, powerlines, railroad tracks, and rivers.

Basin Bowl-shaped depression in the surface of the earth, often shaped by glaciers.

Bear Bag (Bear-bagging) Practice of suspending a food bag in a manner meant to protect it from bears, on a sturdy limb at least fifteen feet from the ground and at least six feet from the trunk.

Bear Bells Safety device worn by hikers to alert bears of their presence.

Bearing, Compass The direction of travel from one point to another. The first point is always true north (or magnetic north if your compass has not been adjusted for declination). A bearing of 90 degrees is to travel directly east. You can also "take a bearing" on an object to see in which direction it lies in relation to your location.

Bed The primary excavated surface of a trail upon which the tread or finished surface lies. Also the bottom of a channel, creek, river, stream, or other body of water.

Bedrock Solid rock material underlying soils and other earthy surface formations.

Benchmark A metal disk set into the ground for use as an exact reference point by surveyors. Bench marks are indicated on a topographic map with an X and the letter BM with an elevation next to it.

Bergschrund Crevasse that separates flowing ice from stagnant ice at the head of a glacier.

Biodiversity The variety and variability within and among living populations and species of organisms and the ecosystems in which they occur.

Biotic Communities The assemblage of native and exotic plants of a particular site or landscape, including microorganisms, fungi, algae, vascular and herbaceous plants, invertebrates, and vertebrates.

Bivouac The site where a tent is set up. To spend a night out without a tent.

Bivouac Sack (Bivvy Sack) A lightweight, unfilled, waterproof bag that can cover a sleeping bag. Also a type of tent for only one person. More colorfully referred to as a "body bag."

Blaze A trail marker. Blazes can be made on a tree by scraping away some of the bark and painting a 2-inch by 6-inch vertical rectangle. Plastic or metal triangles or diamonds (known as blazes) with the name of the trail or a directional arrow imprinted can be purchased and nailed to trees or posts to mark a trail route.

Blaze, Blue The color often used to paint blazes that mark side trails to a campsite or a town off main trails such as the Appalachian Trail. Many other trails follow the Appalachian Trail example.

Blaze, Blue When used as a verb it means to take trails other than the official trail you are on because they offer a shorter or easier alternative to your route.

Blaze, Double (Offset Blazes) Two blazes (vertical alignment) that denote a change in direction or junction in the trail ahead. Usually the top blaze is offset in the direction of the turn.

Blaze, White White blazes are generally used to mark a main or trunk trail such as the Appalachian Trail.

Blazer, Black Someone who removes or paints over trail markers.

Blazer, Blue Thru-hiker who shortcuts the main trail by using connectors and bypasses.

Blazer, Yellow A long-distance trail user taking to the road instead of sticking to the trail.

Bleeder Trail that begins in promising shape but inexplicably vanishes.

Blister The painful result of friction between your foot and boot. As your foot rubs agains the inside of the boot, the point of contact on your foot becomes red and irritated (this is often referred to as a "hot spot") and sure enough, a pocket of fluid—a blister—then develops under the top layer of skin.

Blowdown Trees toppled over by high winds.

Bluff A steep headland, riverbank, or cliff.

Boardwalk An elevated, fixed-planked structure, usually built on pilings in areas of wet soil or water to provide dry crossings.

Bog A mucky or peaty surface soil underlain by peat where little direct sunlight reaches the trail, or where there are flat areas that are difficult to drain.

Bonk When muscles completely run out of fuel and you're tired and spacey. Can be treated by consuming carbohydrate-rich foods.

Boulder A large substrate particle that is larger than cobble.

Boulder (Bouldering) Basic or intermediate climbing carried out on relatively small rocks that can be traversed without great risk of bodily harm in case of a fall.

Boulder Field An area so densely populated by large boulders that the hiker must by necessity walk over—or around—them.

Break-in Period of time necessary for hiking boots or for a piece of equipment to adjust to ideal condition for hiking.

Breathable fabric Special fabric that keeps rain and moisture out while letting body moisture out; Gore-Tex is one of the better known varieties of this fabric.

Bridge A structure, including supports, erected over a depression (stream, river, chasm, canyon, or road) and having a deck for carrying trail traffic. If the bridge is over two feet above the surface, it should have railings.

Bridleway (Bridle Path) Public way designed and maintained primarily for equestrian use. Other non-motorized uses may be permitted.

Brook A small natural stream of water.

Brush Vegetation or small flora.

Brushing To clear the trail corridor of plants, trees, and branches, which could impede the progress of trail users.

Brushing-In (Obliteration) To pile logs, branches, rocks, or duff along the sides of the tread to keep users from widening the trail; or to fill in a closed trail with debris so that it will not be used.

Bug Dope Chemical or botanical substance.

Bump-up Box (Bounce Box, Leapfrog Box, Floater Box) Box containing supplies that a thru-hiker needs but doesn't want to carry (repair kit, batteries, extra glasses, or excess quantities of stuff such as coffee). It is shipped ahead to next resupply point.

Bushwhack Off-trail hiking (originally where the going was difficult, where many bushes had to be whacked). Now it is often used to mean off-trail travel regardless of whether the going is difficult or not.

Butte A conspicuous hill with steep sides and a flat top. The top is usually cap-rock of resistant material. Frequently an erosional remnant in an area of flat-lying sedimentary rock.

Cache A supply of food, water, or tools, usually buried or hidden.

Cadence Stride rate measured in the number of steps you take on average per minute. Comfortable speed is 80 to 120 steps per minute.

Cagoule Long anorak descending below the knees.

Cairn (Duck) A constructed pile of rocks located adjacent to a trail used to mark the route in lieu of a blaze. Often used in open or treeless areas where trail is indistinct.

Call Box An emergency telephone system installed along a trail with direct connection to the local 911 network.

Cameling (Cameling Up) Drinking all the water you can while at a water source, so that you minimize the amount of water you need to carry.

Camp (Campsite, Camping) Living outdoors in a tent or trailer while on vacation or as a recreational activity. Site where overnight stays are permitted.

Camp Host (Campground Host) Many regional, state, and federal campgrounds use volunteer camp hosts whose duties can include checking campers in and out, providing information on the park and its resources, and serving as initial contact for campers in emergency situations.

Camping, Car A means of camping whereby a vehicle, carrying necessary supplies and equipment, is parked overnight in an established campsite.

Camping, Stealth Camping without leaving a trace.

Canal An artificial waterway for transportation or irrigation. Canal and irrigation ditch banks are often used as trails.

Canopy The more or less continuous cover of branches and foliage formed collectively by the crowns of adjacent trees and other woody growth.

Canteen A flask for carrying liquids (as on a hike).

Canyon A long, deep narrow valley with steep cliff walls cut into the earth by running water and often having a creek or river at the bottom.

Cap, Hiker's A close-fitting covering for the head, usually of soft supple material, lacking a brim but often, in its use for hikers, having a visor.

Cape A piece of land extending into water.

Carabiner An oblong metal clip with a spring-loaded gate used to clip slings to ropes or ropes to anchors.

Cartographer A person who draws or makes maps.

Cascade A short, steep drop in streambed elevation often marked by boulders and agitated whitewater.

Cat Hole (Cathole) A hole you dig 6 to 8 inches deep, into which you deposit solid human waste at least 200 feet from water, camp, and trails. Cover and camouflage the cat hole when finished.

Cave Any naturally occurring void, cavity, recess, or system of interconnected passages that occurs beneath the surface of the earth or within a cliff or ledge (including any cave resource therein, but not including any mine, tunnel, aqueduct, or other excavation) and which is large enough to serve as cave habitat for wildlife.

Cavity A hole or hollow place in a tree.

Center Line An imaginary line marking the center of the trail. During construction, the center line is usually marked by placing a row of flags or stakes.

Channel An area that contains continuously or periodically flowing water that is confined by banks and a streambed.

Chigger (Redbug) The tiny, red larva of certain mites. Bites cause itching and red welts.

Cirque A bowl-shaped depression with very steep sides that forms at the head of a mountain glacier. Forms from cold-climate weathering processes including frost.

Cistern A small collection pool constructed from rock or rot-resistant wood to help protect water quality in heavily used areas.

Clear-Cut (Clear-cutting) Removal of all trees and shrubs, not just mature growth.

Clearing Removal of windfall trees, uproots, leaning trees, loose limbs, wood chunks, etc. from both the vertical and horizontal trail corridor.

Clinometer A hand-held instrument used for measuring percent of trail grade. The user sights through the Clinometer to a reference (usually a second person) and reads the measurement directly from the internal scale.

Coastal plain An area of low relief along a continental margin that is underlain by thick, gently dipping sediments.

Col A pass between two mountain peaks; or a low

spot in a mountain ridge.

Compass A direction-indicating device that is used with a map to plot a route or check your position.

Concessionaire A person or business that contracts with a trail operating agency (public or private) to operate a facility or over a service.

Concessions Facilities or services that are leased out to entities other than the trail operator, i.e., sale of food and beverages, accessories, equipment, guided trips, and souvenirs of use or interest to trail users.

Confluence The act of flowing together; the meeting or junction of two or more streams; also, the place where these streams meet. The stream or body of water formed by the junction of two or more streams; a combined flood.

Conifer A tree comprising a wide range of trees that are mostly evergreens. Conifers bear cones (hence, coniferous) and have needle-shaped or scale-like leaves.

Connectors Paths or on-road routes in heavily built environments that provide key connections between or within trail or greenway corridors; often, links from subdivisions or neighborhoods to main trails.

Conservancy A non-profit, privately funded

organization whose purpose is to acquire lands for conservation of natural elements.

Conservation Controlled use and protection of natural resources. The process or means of achieving recovery of variable populations.

Conservation Area Designated land where conservation strategies are applied for the purpose of attaining a viable plant or animal population.

Continental Divide The dividing line for a continent that determines which ocean precipitation will flow into eventually. Every continent except for Antarctica has a continental divide. The Continental Divide in the Americas is the line that divides the flow of water between the Pacific Ocean and Atlantic Ocean.

Contour Line (Contour) A line on a topographic map connecting points of the land surface that have the same elevation.

Contour Map A map that shows the change in value of a variable over a geographic area through the use of contour lines.

Corridor, Scenic Land set aside on either side of a trail to act as a buffer zone protecting the trail against impacts such as logging or development, which would detract from the quality and experience of a trail.

Corridor, Trail The full dimensions of the trail, including the area (2 to 3 feet) on either side of the tread and the space overhead (10 to 12 feet) from which brush and obstacles need to be cleared. The area of passage of the trail, including all cleared and managed parts above, below, and adjacent to the tread.

Counter, Trail-Traffic Used to gather numbers of individuals or groups using a trail. The three most commonly used types of trail-traffic counters are loop-type, photoelectric, and seismic sensor plate counters.

Cover, Ground Vegetation or other material providing protection to a surface; area covered by live above ground parts of plants.

Crampon(s) Spikes that attach to the soles of boots, for traveling on hard snow or ice.

Cranking To hike at a fast pace.

Creek Small body of running water moving in a natural channel or bed.

Creek, Ephemeral A temporary or short-lived water flow only in direct response to a heavy rain. Most of the year it's a dry bed.

Creek, Intermittent Channels that naturally carry water part of the year and are dry the other part.

Creek, Perennial Creek channels that carry water year round.

Creek, Seasonal Channels that naturally carry water part of the year, typically during the winter and spring months, and are dry the other part.

Creek Bank The side slopes of an active channel between which the creek flow is normally confined.

Creek Crossing A trail crossing a body of running water at grade without the use of a developed structure or bridge.

Creekbed The unvegetated portion of a channel boundary below the baseflow water level. The channel through which a natural stream of water runs or used to run, as a dry creekbed.

Crevasse A deep fissure, as in a glacier; a chasm. A crack or breach in a dike or levee.

Cross-Country Travel (Off-Trail Travel) Hiking across open country rather than on a trail.

Cross Training Doing two or more aerobic activities such as hiking, bicycling and swimming on a regular basis.

Crown (Crowning) A method of trail construction where the center portion of the tread is raised to allow water to disperse to either side of the trail.

Cryptosporidiosis A disease of the intestinal tract caused by the parasite Cryptosporidium parvum occurring in untreated backcountry water sources. Common symptoms include stomach cramps and diarrhea.

Cultural Resource(s) The physical remains of human activity (such as artifacts, ruins, burial mounds, petroglyphs, etc.) having scientific, prehistoric, or social values.

Dam A barrier constructed across a waterway to control the flow or raise the level of water. The embankment can be used as a trail to cross a river.

Day Hike A hike that begins and ends during daylight hours.

Day Pack (Daypack) A soft pack (smaller than a backpack), favored by day hikers for carrying food, water, and other supplies.

Deadfall A tangled mass of fallen trees or branches.

Declination The measurement describing the difference between true north and magnetic north.

DEET The active ingredient (chemical name N, N-diethyl-meta-toluamide) used in many insect repellents to repel biting pests such as mosquitoes and ticks.

Dehydration A depletion of body fluids that can hinder the body's ability to regulate its own temperature.

Delta The fan-shaped area at the mouth, or lower end, or a river, formed by eroded material that has been carried downstream and dropped in quantities that can not be carried off by tides or currents.

Descent A downward incline or passage or process of descending from a higher to a lower location.

Descent, First A much-coveted prize; first to descend into a certain canyon or via a certain route.

Difficulty Levels (Ratings) A subjective rating of degree of challenge a trail presents based on an average user with average physical abilities and skills. Difficulty is a function of trail condition and route location factors such as alignment, steepness of grades, gain and loss of elevation, and amount and kind of natural barriers that must be crossed. Snow, ice, rain, and other weather conditions may increase the level of difficulty. For example, some trail providers use Easy, Moderate, Difficult. Many other agencies use the USDA Forest Service levels:

- **Easiest** A trail requiring limited skill with little challenge to travel
- **More Difficult** A trail requiring some skill and challenge to travel.
- **Most Difficult** A trail requiring a high degree of skill and challenge to travel.

Dike (Raised Causeway) A low wall, often of sod, dividing or enclosing lands. The embankment is often used as a trail.

Direction of Travel Arrow The arrow on the base plate of a compass indicating the direction you should hike when you have established a bearing.

Disturbed Area Area where vegetation or topsoil has been removed, or where topsoil, spoil, or waste has been placed.

Divide A ridge that separates two adjacent drainage basins.

Down Insulation for clothing and sleeping bags made from duck or goose feathers.

Down Tree Fallen tree that blocks the trail.

Drainage The way in which water flows downhill and/or off the trail.

Draw Small valley or gap.

Drift Material of any sort deposited by geological processes in one place after having been removed from another. Glacial drift includes the materials deposited by glaciers and by the stream and lakes associated with them.

Drop-off Slope that falls away steeply.

Dry Wash (Sandwash) A streambed that carries water only during and immediately following rainstorms.

Duck (Cairn) A constructed pile of rocks located adjacent to a trail used to mark the route in lieu of a blaze. Often used in open or treeless areas where trail is indistinct.

Dunes Ridges or mounds of loose, wind-blown material, usually sand.

Easement Grants the right to use a specific portion of land for a specific purpose or purposes.

Ecological Corridor(s) Purchased/protected primarily for natural resource protection or wild-life corridors, although they often contain trails or other amenities aimed at serving the human population.

Ecology The branch of biology that deals with the mutual relations among organisms and between organisms and their environment.

Ecosystem A system formed by the interaction of living organisms, including people, with their environment. An ecosystem can be of any size, such as a log, pond, field, forest, or the earth's biosphere.

Eco-Tourism Nature-based tourism. Purposeful travel to natural areas to understand the culture and natural history of the environment, taking care not to alter the integrity of the ecosystem, while producing economic opportunities that make the conservation of natural resources beneficial to local people.

Eddy A current running contrary to the main current, causing water turbulence, e.g., below the bridge pier where swift current is passing through, or below a bar or point.

Elevation The height of a place (mountain or other landmark) given in the number of feet or meters above sea level.

End-to-Ender A person who has traveled the entire distance between termini of a long distance trail.

Endangered species Any plant or animal species that is in danger of extinction throughout all or a significant portion of its range, and has been officially listed as endangered by the Secretary of Interior or Commerce under the provisions of the Endangered Species Act. A final rule for the listing has been published in the Federal Register.

Environment The aggregate of external conditions (physical, biological, economic, and social) that may act upon an organism to influence its development.

Environment, Natural Those parts of the landscape with features more closely resembling what

35

they otherwise would presumably be like if they were left undisturbed by human activities.

Environmental Education Activities that use a structured process to build knowledge, in students and others, about environmental topics.

Environmental Impact The positive or negative effect of any action upon a given area or source.

Equestrian Of horses, horseback riding, riders, and horsemanship.

Erosion Natural processes (water, wind, ice, or other physical processes) by which soil particles are detached from the ground surface and moved downslope, principally by the actions of running water (gully, rill, or sheet erosion).

Escarpment A steep slope or cliff formed by the erosion of the inclined strata of hard rocks.

Estuary A partially enclosed body of water freely connected to the ocean, within which the seawater is diluted by mixing with freshwater and where tidal fluctuations affect river water levels. The estuary is a dynamic system typified by brackish water, variable and often high nutrient levels and by shallow water conditions often associated with marsh plants in upper tidal zones and eelgrass in lower tidal zones.

Evaporative Heat Loss When you sweat, you

lose heat through the evaporation of the liquid. This is great in warm weather because it cools the body; but when it is cold and once you stop moving, your clothes remain wet, which can lead to chilling.

Exotic Species A plant introduced from another country or geographic region outside its natural range.

Face The steep exposed side of a rock.

Face Plant A face-first tumble.

False Summit A high point that seems to be the summit until you get close enough to see that you are not yet done climbing.

Fanny Pack A waist pack, especially as worn with the pouch over the buttocks.

Fastpacker Anyone who passes you on the trail.

Fault A fracture in rock along which movement can be demonstrated. A fracture in the earth's crust forming a boundary between rock masses that have shifted.

Fauna The animal populations and species of a specified region.

Federal Land Land owned by the United States, without reference to how the land was acquired or which Federal Agency administers the land.

Feng Shui (pronounced "fung shway") Literally meaning wind and water. The Chinese art and science of arranging spaces and elements in the space (in or outdoor) to create harmonious energy flows and patterns, tempering or enhancing the energy where necessary. Some trail designers use Feng Shui.

Fire Ring Circle of rocks or metal ring used to contain a fire. A proper fire ring is constructed to prevent the spread of fire above and below ground level. You should only use fire rings found in designated sites.

Fire Road Unimproved dirt road that allows fire fighting and ranger vehicles access to the backcountry.

Firebreak A strip of forest, prairie land or mountain slope cleared or plowed to stop or prevent the spread of fire.

Flagging Thin ribbon used for marking during the location, design, construction, or maintenance of a trail project.

Flash Flood A sudden flood of great volume, usually caused by a heavy rain. Also, a flood that crests in a short length of time and is often characterized by high velocity flows.

Flashlight A small portable lamp usually powered by batteries.

Flip-Flop To travel on a long distance trail continuously, time-wise but not necessarily in the same direction. For example, you might flip-flop by traveling north then skipping a section of trail and traveling south until you get to where you left off.

Floodplain (Flood Plain) Flat, occasionally flooded areas, bordering streams, rivers, or other bodies of water, susceptible to changes in the surface level of the water. Floodplains are formed of fluvial sediments and are periodically flooded and modified when streams overflow.

Flora The plant populations and species of a specified region.

Flow The rhythm or "feel" of a trail. Two basic types include "open and flowing" and "tight and technical."

Footpath A path over which the public has a right-of-way on foot only.

Ford A natural water level stream crossing. Can be improved to provide a level, low velocity surface for trail traffic.

Forest Canopy The combination of upper branches and leaves of trees (tree crowns) in an area.

Freshet Sudden overflow of a creek or stream caused by a heavy rain or by thawing snow and ice.

Friends of the Trail A private, non-profit organization formed to advocate and promote a trail. They can provide assistance, whether muscle power or political power, that augments management of a trail by a public agency.

Frostbite The freezing of skin and the tissue beneath.

Frostline The maximum depth that frost can be expected to penetrate into the ground.

Gaiters (Leggings, Puttees) Coverings that zip or snap around the ankles and lower legs to keep debris and water out of your boots.

Game Any species of fish or wildlife for which state or federal laws and regulations proscribe hunting seasons and bag or creel limits.

Gear, Hiking Clothes and accessories used for hiking.

Geocaching Involves hiding a cache (a stash of goods and a log book) in a remote location and recording its location using a GPS unit. The coordinates, along with a few helpful hints, are then posted on a website for other GPS-wielding geo-cachers to look up and then hunt for a cache; a modern day treasure hunt.

Geographic Information System (GIS) A spatial database mapping system (computer and software) that contains location data for trails and other important features.

Giardiasis An intestinal illness (diarrhea, excessive gas, and abdominal cramping) caused by the protozoan parasite Giardia lamblia occurring in untreated backcountry water sources.

Glacier A huge mass of ice, formed on land by the compaction and re-crystallization of snow, that moves very slowly down slope or outward due to its own weight.

Glade An open space in a forest.

Glen A narrow, deep and often secluded mountain valley, especially in Scotland or Ireland.

Glissade To slide down a snow slope, either sitting or standing, using an ice-axe to control speed and direction.

Global Positioning System (GPS) A system used to map trail locations using satellites and portable receivers. Data gathered can be downloaded directly into GIS database systems.

Gore-Tex A trademark used for a water-repellant, breathable laminated fabric with a micro-thin membrane used primarily in outerwear, tents, and hiking boots.

Gorge A deep narrow passage with steep rocky sides; a ravine.

GORP The original high-carbohydrate trail snack made primarily from nuts and dried fruit, an acronym for "Good Ol' Raisins and Peanuts."

Grade The vertical distance of ascent or descent of the trail expressed as a percentage of the horizontal distance, commonly measured as a ratio of rise to length or as a percent. For example, a trail that rises 8 vertical feet in 100 horizontal feet has an 8 percent grade.

Grade, Average Trail (Overall Trail Grade) The average steepness of a trail over its entire length.

Grade, Change of An abrupt difference between the grade of two adjacent surfaces.

Grade, Maximum The steepest grade permitted on any part of a trail.

Grade, Negative Trail runs downhill.

Grade, Percent of Preferred method of measuring slope, or a hill's steepness. For example, a grade of 10 percent means there is a rise or fall of 10 vertical feet per 100 linear feet.

Grade, Positive Trail runs uphill.

Grass (Forbs) Herbaceous vegetation.

Gravel Rock fragments ranging from 1/5 to 3 inches in diameter.

Great Hiking Era The period between 1890 and 1930 was such a wonderful time to hit the trail that historians in some parts of the U.S., particularly in California, refer to it as "The Great Hiking Era." Many trail camps and small-scale resorts were established during these decades and mountainous regions were crisscrossed with trails.

Green An open space available for unstructured recreation consisting of grassy areas and trees.

Greenbelt A series of connected open spaces that may follow natural features such as ravines, creeks, or streams. May surround cities and serve to conserve and direct urban and suburban growth.

Greenhorn Inexperienced hiker.

Greenspace Natural areas, open spaces, trails, and greenways that function for both wildlife and people.

Greenway A linear open space established along a natural corridor, such as a river, stream, ridgeline, rail-trail, canal, or other route for conservation, recreation, or alternative transportation purposes.

Green Exercise Physical activities that give participants the benefits of exercise and direct exposure to nature. Hikers are the chief practitioners of green exercise, also practiced by kayakers, surfers and cross-country skiers.

Green Tunnel An older nickname for the Appalachian Trail, so named because much of it leads beneath a canopy of trees.

Grid A pattern of squares on a map that help find features or fix position. Coordinate numbers for horizontal and vertical lines can be traced to an intersection in a particular grid.

Groundwater Water that infiltrates through the ground surface and accumulates in underground water bodies in porous rock or gravels.

Grub (Grubbing) Removal of roots, stumps, rocks, soil, etc., from the trail tread and corridor.

Guardrail A 36- to 42-inch high railing for guarding against danger at the edge of a deck, bridge, or boardwalk to prevent people from falling.

Gulf A large inlet of water surrounded by land; usually surrounded on three sides by land. Larger than a bay.

Gully-washer Heavy rain.

Guzzler A water development for wildlife that relies on rainfall or snowmelt to recharge it, rather than springs or streams. Usually used where no other sources of wildlife water exist.

Habitat A place that supports a plant or animal population because it supplies that organism's basic requirements of food, water, shelter, living space, and security.

Hammock A cluster of trees, often hardwoods on higher ground.

Hantavirus A respiratory disease that is carried in wild rodents such as deer mice. People become infected after breathing airborne particles of urine or saliva found in rodent-infested areas. The virus produces flu-like symptoms and takes one to five weeks to incubate. It is 60 percent fatal.

Harmony A combination of parts into a pleasing or orderly whole: congruity; a state of agreement of proportionate arrangement of form, line, color, and texture.

Hat, Hiker's A covering for the head, especially one with a shaped crown and brim.

Headlamp A light source worn affixed to the head for outdoor activities at night or in dark conditions for hiking and camping. Often substitutes for a flashlight in the Ten Essentials.

Headland A narrow area of land jutting out into a sea or lake.

Headwaters The area in the upper reaches of a watershed typified by unconfined surface water flows. Headwaters can coalesce to form rivulets or first order streams with distinct channels.

Headwaters can often be ephemeral (wet only part of the year).

Heat Exhaustion Body's reaction to overheating, which includes salt-deficiency and dehydration.

Heatstroke A severe illness in which the body's temperature rises way above normal; also called sunstroke.

Height Measure of the vertical dimension of a feature. May also be the depth of a rut or dip.

Herbaceous Plants that are green and leaf like in appearance or texture and have characteristics typical of an herb, as distinguished from a woody plant.

Heritage Resource A site, structure, object, or group of sites or structures used or created by people in the past.

Hike To walk in nature. Also, a walk in the mountains or other natural landscape for pleasure.

Hiker One who hikes (especially frequently); a foot traveler; someone who goes on a walk in the mountains or other natural landscape for pleasure.

Hike-ku A hiking-themed haiku, a form of Japanese verse, written in 17 syllables divided into three lines of 5, 7 and 5 syllables, and employing highly evocative allusions and comparison, often on the subject of nature.

Hiking Walking for pleasure in the mountains or other natural landscape.

Hiking Boots Footwear specifically designed for hiking. Considered the most important hiking gear because their fit and quality can assist or impede a hiker's speed, comfort and safety. Good hiking boots protect the hiker's feet against all manner of natural obstacles and provide comfort for walking over rough and uneven terrain.

Hip Belt A belt on a backpack or day pack that straps around the hips, and helps transfer weight from shoulders and back to hips.

Hogback A rounded ridge.

Hostel A low-cost establishment usually offering bunks, showers, and sometimes meals or kitchen facilities to travelers.

Hot Spring A natural spring that delivers water to the surface that is of higher temperature than the human body.

Hump A low mound of earth; a hummock. A mountain range.

Hydration Bag Water bag fitted with a hose through which you can drink, usually carried on your back.

Hyperthermia Unusually high body temperature.

Hypothermia Lowering of the body's core temperature to dangerous levels. Wet conditions, wind, and exhaustion can bring on hypothermia.

Interpretation Communicating information about the natural and/or cultural resources and their associated stories and values found at a specific site or along a trail. Tours, signs, brochures, and other means can be used to interpret a particular resource.

Interpreter Usually in state, national and regional parklands, an employee who explains an area's cultural and natural history via guided tours, trail walks, campfire programs, etc.

Interpretive Display An educational display usually in an interpretive center or at a trailhead that describes and explains a natural or cultural point of interest on or along the trail.

Intersection (Junction) Area where two or more trails or roads join together.

Jerky Meat cut into strips, salted and dried or smoked with low heat. The result is a salty savory snack that can be stored for a long time without refrigeration.

Journey The act of traveling from one place to

another; a trip. Distance to be traveled or time required for trip.

Junction (Intersection) Area where two or more trails or roads join together

Kiosk (Sign) A freestanding bulletin board consisting of three to five sides housing informational or interpretive displays.

Knob Prominent rounded hill or summit on a longer ridge.

Lagoon A shallow area of water separated from the ocean by a sandbank or by a strip of low land.

Lake Large inland body of water.

Land The total natural and cultural environment of the solid surface of the earth.

Land, Private Land owned by a farmer, corporation, or individual (private landowner).

Land, Public Federal, state, or municipal land in trust for the governed populace (public landowner).

Land Ethic The desire humans have to conserve, protect, and respect the native landscape and other natural resources because their own well being is dependent upon the proper functioning of the ecosystem.

Land Management Agency Any agency or organization that manages lands, many managed as recreation and/or wilderness areas. Examples include federal agencies such as the USDA Forest Service, the USDI National Park Service, and the USDI Bureau of Land Management, as well as state, county, and local park system agencies, plus organizations such as The Nature Conservancy.

Land Manager Any person who makes decisions regarding land use.

Land Trust A private, nonprofit conservation organization formed to protect natural resources such as forestland, natural areas, and recreational areas. Land trusts purchase and accept donations of conservation easements.

Landing The transition area on a switchback.

Landmark Any monument or material mark or fixed object used to designate the location of a land boundary on the ground. Any prominent object on land that can be used in determining a location or a direction.

Landscape The sum total of the characteristics that distinguish a certain kind of area on the earth's surface and give it a distinguishing pattern in contrast to other kinds of areas.

Landslide Dislodged rock or earth that has slipped

downhill under the influence of gravity and obstructs passage on a trail.

Latitude The angular distance north or south of the equator, measured in degrees, minutes, and seconds.

Layering Just like it sounds, the hiker adds layers of clothing to stay warm and removes layers to cool off. What makes the concept seem so complex, however, is the dizzying array of fabrics and types of apparel available to hikers.

Layover Day A rest day during an extended hiking or backpacking trip.

Leave No Trace (LNT) Educational program designed to instill behaviors in the outdoors that leave minimum impact of human activities or occupation. Leg In popular usage, this part of the body extends from the top of the thigh down to the foot. However, in the medical profession, the leg refers to the portion of the lower extremity from the knee to the ankle. Also a section or portion of a hike or trail.

Legend A listing that shows symbols and other information about a map.

Leisure The free or discretionary time available for people to use as they choose after meeting the biological and subsistence requirements of existence.

Levee An embankment raised to prevent a river from overflowing. A small ridge or raised area bordering an irrigated field. The embankment is often used as a trail.

Litter The uppermost layer of decaying matter in any plant community (leaf matter), or carelessly discarded trash on the trail.

Livestock Domestic animals kept or raised for food, by-products, work, transportation, or recreation.

L.L. Bean Founded in 1912 in Maine by Leon Leonwood Bean, a source for quality outdoor equipment and apparel.

Loam An easily crumbled soil consisting of a mixture of clay, silt, and sand.

Loft The upper floor of a hiker's shelter often accessed via a ladder. Or, the degree of fluffiness in the fill of a sleeping bag.

Log, Trail An inventory of physical features along or adjacent to a trail. An item-by-item, foot-by-foot record of trail features and structures and the improvements needed on a specific trail.

Longitude The angular distance east or west of the prime meridian, measured in degrees.

Low-impact Camping Camping that does not damage or change the land. Campers leave no sign that they were on the land.

Lowland A relatively flat area in the lower levels of regional elevation.

Lyme Disease An infection caused by a spiral-shaped bacterium called a spirochete carried by deer ticks. Symptoms associated with the early stages include fever, headache, stiffness, lethargy, and myriad other mild complaints—often dismissed as the flu. If left untreated, Lyme disease can produce lifelong impairment of muscular and nervous systems.

Machine Built Trail or feature constructed with the use of an excavator, trail dozer, or other piece of equipment.

Magnetic North A spot in northern Canada, overlying the earth's magnetic North Pole, toward which the red needle of a compass points.

Maildrop Food or sundry resupplies sent to yourself via USPS, UPS, or other carriers. There could be several maildrops on a long-distance trail trip.

Maintainer A volunteer who maintains a section of trail as part of a trail-maintenance program of a trail organization.

Maintenance Repair, improvements, or other work that is carried out on or near a trail to keep a trail in its originally constructed serviceable condition or to improve the safety and sustainability of the site. Usually limited to minor repair or improvements that do not significantly change the trail location, width, surface, or structures.

Maintenance (Annual) Involves four tasks done annually or more often as needed: cleaning drainage, clearing blowdowns, brushing, and marking.

Management Include the over-all policy, planning, design, inventorying, mapping, construction, and maintenance of trail, as well as the operational aspects of administration.

Management Area An area selected for management of an emphasized natural resource, and common management objectives.

Manager The person who has charge of a piece of land (i.e. a Park Manager).

Map A representation on a plane surface, at an established scale, of the physical features (natural, artificial, or both) of a part or the whole of the earth's surface, by means of signs and symbols, and with the means of orientation indicated.

Map Scale The relationship between distance on a map and the distance on the earth's surface.

Marker, Trail An appropriate and distinctive symbol with the name of the trail imprinted on plastic or metal triangles or diamonds and used to mark a trail route.

Marsh A mineral wetland that is permanently or seasonally inundated by standing or slow moving water. The waters are nutrient rich and the substrate is usually mineral soil. Marshes are characterized by communities of emergent rushes, grasses and reeds, and submerged or floating aquatic plants in areas of open water.

Massif A group of mountains.

McLeod A forest fire tool that looks like an oversized hoe with tines on the opposite blade. In trail work it is used to remove slough and berm from a trail and to smooth the tread. The head can also be used for tamping soil.

Meadow Tract of grassland.

Meander To proceed by or take a winding or indirect course. To wander aimlessly; ramble. A winding trail or course. The winding of a stream channel, usually in an erodible alluvial valley.

Measuring Wheel (Cyclometer) A device that records the revolutions of a wheel and hence the distance traveled by the wheel on a trail or land surface.

Mesa Flat-topped elevation with one or more cliff-like sides.

Mileage Crazy (Mileage Craziness) A serious condition that exists in many forms. It can hit travelers while driving, riding in planes, bicycling, or hiking. The symptoms are placing more importance on how many miles are traveled than on the real reason for traveling—to enjoy the journey.

Moleskin Heavy cotton fabric woven and sheared to create a soft pile on one side and used in adhesive pads stuck to the feet to prevent blisters; "Dr. Scholl's" is a well-known moleskin.

Moraine A ridge or pile of boulders, stones, and other debris carried along and deposited by a glacier. Most common moraines are end (or terminal) moraines and lateral (or side) moraines.

Mountaineering (Mountain Climbing, Alpinism) Climbing high mountains (for sport) where skill and gear to enable belaying, rappelling, glacier travel, and climbing over rock, snow, and ice are needed. The object is to reach summits and not simply to traverse trails and passes.

Mouse Trapeze String hung from shelter ceiling with tin can lid above food bag to deter mice from getting at food.

Mouth The exit or point of discharge of a stream into another stream, lake, or sea.

Mud Season A "fifth season," particularly in

northern New England, sometimes extending from about mid-March to Memorial Day, characterized by muddy conditions and sometimes accompanying psychic misery.

Multiple Use A land management objective that seeks to coordinate several environmental, recreational, economic, historical, cultural and/or social values in the same geographic area in a compatible and sustainable manner.

Multiple Use Trail Network A series of trails that interconnect to form a system that, as a whole, allows for more than one use. The individual trails may be single use or multiple use.

National Conservation Area (NCA) Similar to National Monument status; applies solely to BLM lands. Granted only by Congress. These areas provide for the conservation, use, enjoyment, and enhancement of certain natural, recreational, paleontological, and other resources, including fish and wildlife habitat. Individual site determines allowable recreational activities.

National Forest or Grassland System All national forest lands and grasslands reserved or withdrawn from the public domain of the United States. Government officials decide upon appropriate resource extraction such as logging, mining, and oil and gas drilling, as well as appropriate recreational uses such as hiking, mountain biking, hunting, fishing, snowmobiling, and OHVs.

National Historic Trail (NHT) Federally designated extended trails, which closely follow original routes of nationally significant travel (explorers, emigrants, traders, military, etc.). NHTs do not have to be continuous, can be less than 100 miles in length, and can include land and water segments. The Iditarod, the Lewis and Clark, the Mormon Pioneer, and the Oregon trails were the first to be designated as NHTs in 1978.

National Monument Area of unique ecological, geological, historic, prehistoric, cultural, or scientific interest administered by the National Park Service, United States Department of Interior. Traditionally used for historic structures or landmarks on government land; more recently used to grant national park-like status to tracts of western land. Designated by Congress or the president. Individual site determines allowable recreational activities.

National Park Designated primarily to protect resources and recreation opportunities administered by the National Park Service, United States

Department of Interior. Do not allow hunting, mining, or other extractive uses.

National Preserve Often linked with a national park. Some national preserves are administered very much like national parks while others allow mineral and fuel extraction, hunting, and trapping.

National Recreation Area Federal areas that have outstanding combinations of outdoor recreation opportunities, aesthetic attractions, and proximity to potential users. They may also have cultural, historical, archaeological, pastoral, wilderness, scientific, wildlife, and other values contributing to public enjoyment. Designated by Congress. Individual location determines allowable recreational activities.

National Recreation Trail (NRT) Existing trails that provide a variety of outdoor recreation uses in or reasonably accessible to urban areas recognized by the federal government (Secretary of Interior or Secretary of Agriculture, not Congressional action) as contributing to the National Trails System.

National Scenic Area Area that contains outstanding scenic characteristics, recreational values, and geological, ecological, and cultural resources.

National Scenic Trail (NST) Federally designated extended trails (over 100 miles in length), which provide for the maximum outdoor recreation potential and for the conservation and enjoyment of the significant scenic, historic, natural, or cultural qualities of the areas through which they pass. The Appalachian and the Pacific Crest trails were the first to be designated as National Scenic Trails in 1968.

National Seashore Coastal equivalent of a national park.

National Trails System A network of trails (National Scenic, Historic, or Recreation) throughout the country authorized by the 1968 National Trails System Act.

National Trails System Act (NSTA) Was passed as Public Law 90-543, signed by President Johnson on October 2, 1968, after several years of negotiations. It has been amended many times since.

National Wildlife Refuge Preserves wildlife habitat. Allows hunting and fishing; some allow overnight camping.

Native Species An indigenous species (a basic unit of taxonomy) that is normally found as part of a particular ecosystem; a species that was present in a particular area at the time of the Public Land Survey (1847-1907).

Natural Bridge An arch-shaped rock formation

produced by weathering and/or erosion.

Natural History The study and description of organisms and natural objects, especially their origins, evolution, and interrelationships.

Natural Resource(s) For outdoor recreation include areas of land, bodies of water, forests, swamps, and other natural features which are in demand for outdoor recreation or are likely to become so.

Nature The world of living things and the outdoors. The material world and its phenomena. The forces and processes that produce and control all the phenomena of the material world. A primitive state of existence, untouched and uninfluenced by civilization or artificiality.

Nature Deficit Disorder A term coined by author Richard Louv in his 2005 book, "Last Child in the Woods," it refers to the decreasing amount of time children spend outdoors that may result in a wide range of physical, mental and behavioral problems. The term is applicable to adults as well.

Nonmotorized Trail recreation by modes such as hiking, biking, horseback riding, skiing, etc.

Old-growth A forest or woodland characterized by the presence of large old trees, nunmerous snags, woody debris and that is usually in a late stage of ecological succession.

Open Space Areas of natural quality, either publicly or privately owned, designated for protection of natural resources, nature-oriented outdoor recreation, or trail-related activities. In urban settings areas of land not covered by structures, driveways, or parking lots.

Orienteering A sport in which competitors must find their way across country using a map and compass.

Outcrop A rock formation that protrudes through the level of the surrounding soil.

Outdoor Recreation Leisure activities involving the enjoyment and use of natural resources primarily outdoors.

Outerwear Clothing such as jackets, parkas, vests, hats and gloves for use outdoors. This apparel is the outermost layer of a hiker's layering scheme.

Overstory The uppermost layer of foliage that forms a forest canopy.

Pace The rate of movement for a hiker, often expressed in miles per hour.

Park Any area that is predominately open space with natural vegetation and landscaping used principally for active or passive recreation.

Park, Linear A linear open space established along a natural corridor, such as a river, stream, ridgeline, rail-trail, canal, or other route for passive recreation, education, and scenic purposes.

Pass Narrow low spot between mountain peaks; lowest point along a mountain crest. Pass is generally used in the West, while "gap" is used in the South, and "notch" in New England.

Passing Space A section of trail wide enough to allow two users to pass one another or travel abreast.

Path (Pathway) This is a temporary or permanent area that is normally dirt or gravel, although some paths are asphalt or concrete. A path typically indicates the common route taken by pedestrians between two locations.

Pathfinder One that discovers a way; explores untraveled regions to mark a new route. Someone who promotes a new process or procedure.

Peak The high point of a mountain or hill.

Peak-Bagging Reaching the tops of as many peaks as possible and keeping a record of the accomplishment.

Pedestrian Any person traveling by foot, or any mobility-impaired person using a wheelchair, whether manually operated or motorized.

Peninsula A piece of land extending into the sea almost surrounded by water.

Peripatetic Walking about; moving from place to place.

Permit (System) Use-authorization forms issued by agencies to control the amount of use along trails or in wilderness areas. Permits may be obtained from the agency office, by mail, over the phone, online, or in person, or they may be self-issued; self-issued permits are usually obtained at the trailhead or immediately outside agency offices. They can be used to increase visitor knowledge about regulations, recommended low-impact behaviors, and potential hazards.

Physical Feature A land shape formed by nature.

Picnic Area Day-use area with one or more picnic tables where meals can be eaten outdoors.

Pilgrimage A journey to a sacred place or shrine. Often a long journey or search, and one of exalted purpose and moral/religious significance.

Pitch An increase in the prevailing grade of a trail.

Piton A spike (driven into rock) to which ropes are attached during climbing or rigging.

Plateau An elevated area of mostly level land, sometimes containing deep canyons.

Playa The usually dry and very level lake-plain that

occupies the lowest part of a closed depression.

Poach (Poacher) To nab a campsite without a permit.

Point(s) of Interest Ecological, historic, cultural, and recreational features or sites that may contribute to the quality of a trail user's experience.

Poison ivy A North American shrub or vine that has compound leaves with three leaflets, small green flowers and whitish berries that cause a rash on contact. Also a skin rash caused by contact with this plant.

Poison oak A shrub or vine that has compound leaves and three lobed leaflets that grows in western North America, primarily west of the Rocky Mountains. Also a skin rash caused by contact with this plant.

Pond Still body of water smaller than a lake, often artificially formed, that is shallow enough to permit sunlight to reach the bottom, thus allowing plant growth.

Pool A reach of a stream that is characterized by deep, low-velocity water and a smooth surface.

Porta-potty Portable toilet.

Post-hole To punch through deep snow with each step.

Potable (Water) Safe to drink from the source without treating.

Power Hiker One who covers long distances, often with significant elevation gain, often beginning before sunrise and hiking until dusk.

Prescribed Burns Formerly called "controlled burns," these are periodic, intentional fires used to clear underbrush in an effort to control wildfires, open areas to wildlife, and promote germination of some species of flora.

Preservation Maintaining an area or structure intact or unchanged.

Privy Outhouse or latrine.

Prime Meridian An imaginary line running from north to south through Greenwich, England, uses as the reference point for longitude.

Primitive Characterized by an essentially unmodified natural environment isolated from the sights, sounds, and structures of civilization.

Pristine A place where signs of human impacts are absent or difficult to detect.

Promontory A prominent mass of land overlooking or projecting into or above a lowland. A high point of land or rock projecting into a body of water.

Public Land Any land and interest in land owned

by the United States and administered by the Secretary of the Interior through the Bureau of Land Management.

Pulaski During the early 1900s US Forest Service Ranger Edward Pulaski of Idaho needed a good tool for grubbing and chopping fire lines, so he welded the blade of a pick to the back of an ax head and created what has come to be known as the "Pulaski." The modern Pulaski combines an axe bit with an adz-shaped grub hoe and is a very popular tool among trail builders.

Purifier Usually refers to a filter that employs an iodine-impregnated medium to kill water-borne organisms too small to be filtered out.

Quadrangle A tract of land represented by one US Geological Survey map sheet.

Quality-of-Life Term used to embrace many facets of life and community (culture, density, climate, etc.). Recreation, parks, open space, and trail opportunities play an important role in a community's quality-of-life.

Radiant Heat Loss Is when heat radiates out from your body into your clothes. Vapor barriers reflect the heat back to your body.

Rail-Trail (Rail-to-Trail) A multi-purpose, public path or trail (paved or natural) created along an inactive railroad corridor.

Rain Water falling to earth in drops that have been condensed from moisture in the atmosphere.

Ranger The keeper of a park, preserve or forest, who protects the land and its visitors and enforces the law.

Rapid(s) An area of broken, fast-flowing water in a stream, where the slope of the bed increases (but without a prominent break of slope which might result in a waterfall), or where a gently dipping bar of harder rock outcrops.

Rappel (Roping Down) Self-belaying down a length of rope to get down from a steep climb.

Rare Plant or animal species that are uncommon in a specific area. All endangered, threatened, and sensitive species can be considered rare, but the converse is not true.

Ravine Deep, narrow gouge in the earth's surface, usually eroded by the flow of water.

Recreation The refreshment of body and mind through forms of play, amusement, or relaxation; usually considered any type of conscious enjoyment that occurs during leisure time.

Recreation, Developed Outdoor recreation

requiring significant capital investment in
facilities to handle a concentration of visitors
on a relatively small area. Examples are ski areas,
resorts, trailheads, and campgrounds.

Recreation, Dispersed Outdoor recreation activities that occur outside of developed recreation
facilities in which visitors are diffused over relatively large areas away from maintained roads. Also
referred to as backcountry recreation.

Recreation, Passive Outdoor Recreational uses
conducted almost wholly outdoors that generally
do not require a developed site, including hiking,
horseback riding, and bird-watching.

Recreation Site, Developed A site developed
primarily to accommodate specific intensive use
activities or groupings of activities such as hiking, camping, picnicking, boating, swimming,
and more.

REI (Recreational Equipment Inc.) Large U.S.
corporation, a leader in the outdoor recreation
industry, that sells gear via retail stores in about
30 states and online.

Recreational Trails Program (RTP) Federal
program first established in 1991, RTP returns
a portion of federal gasoline taxes, generated by
non-highway recreation, to the states, which in

turn provide grants for trail-related purposes to private organizations, state and federal agencies, and municipalities.

Re-entry Physical, mental and emotional process of a hiker (often a long-distance one) re-adjusting to modern life and its pace after a hike.

Reforestation The natural or artificial regeneration of an area to protect watersheds, prevent soil erosion, improve wildlife habitat and other natural resources, produce timber and other wood products, and restore function to a particular type ecosystem.

Register, Trail Along long-distance trails you may find "trail registers" at overnight stops or trailheads that allow users the chance to make comments to those behind them, and read comments from those ahead. Registers can be an important safety measure to pinpoint the location of trail users.

Registration, Trail A survey form filled out and left at a trailhead drop box or office that allows managers to obtain use information. Or a required permit to use a trail.

Relief Elevations or depressions of the land.

Relocation (Relo, Realignment, Reroute) To alter the path of an existing trail to better follow land contours, avoid drainage sites, bypass environmentally sensitive areas, improve views, or for other landowner or management reasons.

Reserve(s) Large protected areas that serve as primary sites for the conservation of biological diversity, natural resources, and in some cases for important archaeological and historic sites.

Rest Step An uphill hiking technique where with each step, the rearmost leg is locked completely straight momentarily shifting weight from leg muscles to leg bones giving muscles a very short moment of complete rest.

Restroom (Comfort Station, Pit Privy, Chum Privy, Vault Toilet, Composting Toilet, Chemical Toilet, Port-a-John, Latrine, Bathhouse) Facility for human waste disposal that may or may not meet public health standards.

Ridge A hill that is proportionally longer than it is wide, generally with steeply sloping sides.

Ridgeline A line connecting the highest points along a ridge and separating drainage basins or small-scale drainage systems from one another.

Ridgerunner A person paid to travel and oversee a specific section of trail.

Right-of-Way A linear corridor of land held in fee simple title, or as an easement over another's land, for use as a public utility (highway, road, railroad, trail, utilities, etc.) for a public purpose.

Right of Way The right of one trail user to proceed in a lawful manner in preference to another trail user.

Riparian (Riparian Zone, Habitat Zone) A habitat that is strongly influenced by water and that occurs adjacent to streams, shorelines, wetlands, or other water bodies, dominated by high soil moisture content and influenced by adjacent upland vegetation.

Riparian Vegetation Plant species growing adjacent to a wetland area, including a perennial or intermittent stream, lake, river, pond, spring, marsh, bog, meadow, etc.

River Large natural streams that continuously or periodically contain moving water, or which form a connection between two bodies of water.

Riverine Relating to, formed by, or resembling a river including tributaries, streams, brooks, etc.

Road A vehicle route that has been improved and maintained by mechanical means to ensure relatively regular and continuous use.

Road-to-Trail Conversion Involves narrowing an old road (typically former logging, mining or fire roads) to provide a meandering trail with a solid trail tread for users.

Rock Soil particles greater than 3 inches in diameter.

Rock Art (Petroglyph or Pictograph) An archaic to modern cultural site type consisting of incised (petroglyph) or painted (pictograph) figures such as people, animals, plants, or abstracts on a rock surface.

Roller-coaster Section of trail with constant ups and downs.

Route A traveled way, a means of access, a line of travel, an established or selected course of travel.

Runoff Water (not absorbed by the soil) that flows over the land surface and ultimately reaches streams.

Rural Usually refers to areas with population less than 5,000.

Saddle Ridge between two peaks.

Salt Marsh An area of low-lying, wet ground containing a high proportion of salt or alkali; generally in arid regions.

Saunter A leisurely pace. A leisurely walk or hike.

Savannah A flat, almost treeless grassland.

Scale The proportionate size relationship between an object and the surroundings in which the object is placed. The relationship of the length between two points as shown on a map and the distance between the same two points on the Earth.

Scenery The aggregate of features that give character to a landscape.

Scenic Viewpoint A designated area developed at a key location to afford trail users an opportunity to view significant landforms, landscape features, wildlife habitat, and activities.

Scour (Scouring) Soil erosion through the force of moving water.

Screamer A long fall.

Scree (Scree Slope) Gravel-size loose rock debris, especially on a steep slope or at the base of a cliff, formed as a result of disintegration largely by weathering.

Sea Level The ocean surface; the mean level between high and low tides. Sea level is used as a reference point in determining land elevation.

Section Nominally one-mile by one-mile area of land bounded by section lines running east-west and north-south.

Section-hiker A hiker who is hiking an entire trail over a period of years.

Sediment Soil particles that have been transported away from their natural location by wind or water action and re-deposited in a different area down-slope or down-stream.

Self-Arrest Ice-axe technique used to stop yourself from sliding off a icy mountainside. You use your body weight to plunge the serrated blade of the axe into the icy mountainside; ideally you find yourself halted midslope.

Semiarid Moderately dry; region or climate where moisture is normally greater than under arid conditions but still definitely limits the production of vegetation.

Shelter (Adirondack, Lean-To, Stone, Log) Open front structure that includes a sleeping platform and roof; popular as an overnight facility on long-distance trails, especially in the East.

Sherpa(s) A member of the Himalayan people living in Nepal and Tibet who are famous for their skill as mountaineers. In modern times Sherpas have achieved world renown as expert guides on Himalayan mountaineering expeditions. To carry another's gear, as in, "I Sherpaed both of our packs the entire morning."

Shore That part of the land in immediate contact with a body of water including the area between high and low water lines.

Shoreline The line of contact between a body of water and the land.

Shrub A woody plant that usually remains low and produces shoots or trunks from the base; it is not usually tree-like or single stemmed.

Shuttle Leaving a vehicle at both ends of a point-to-point trip or pre-arranging a shuttle to pick you up at the end of the trip or to drop you off at the beginning.

Sight Line (Sight Distance) The visible and unobstructed forward and rear view seen by a trail user from a given point along the trail.

Sign (Signage) A board, post, or placard that displays written, symbolic, tactile, or pictorial information about the trail or surrounding area. Signage increases safety and comfort on trails. There are five basic types of signs: Cautionary, Directional, Interpretive, Objective, Regulatory.

Sign, Cautionary Warns of upcoming roadway crossings, steep grades, blind curves, and other potential trail hazards.

Sign, Directional Gives street names, trail names, direction arrows, mileage to points of interest, and other navigational information.

Sign, Interpretive Offers educational information that describes and explains a natural or cultural point of interest on or along the trail.

Sign, Objective Provides information about the actual trail conditions, including grade, cross slope, surface, clear trail width, and obstacle height. This allows users to make more informed decisions about which trails best meet their trail needs and abilities.

Sign, Regulatory Tells the "rules of the trail" by prohibiting certain uses or controlling direction of travel.

Sinkhole A natural occurrence when the limestone crust of the earth collapses and creates a crater. Old sinkholes are often filled with water and resemble ponds.

Sinks A term given to areas where underground rivers emerge at the ground surface. Areas surrounding sinks are generally lush with vegetation.

Site Physical location of a place. A parcel of land bounded by a property line or a designated portion of public right of way.

Skirt To work your way around a mountain, wetland or other obstacle. A trail that goes around a mountain, often at an even grade, instead of climbing over the mountain. Also a trail that travels around a sensitive natural feature, such as a wetland, rather than going across it.

Slackpack (Slackpacking, Slackpacker, Bare-backing, Barebacker) Hiking a section of a long distance trail without a backpack by either leaving it in a safe place or having someone shuttle it up the trail for you. This allows you to pack only a few pounds of essentials that suffice until you're met by outside support each night.

Slide Material that has slid onto the trail tread; possibly in quantities sufficient to block the trail.

Slip The downslope movement of a mass of soil under wet or saturated conditions; a micro-landslide.

Slope Rising or falling natural (or created) incline of the land, as shown on contour maps. Generally refers to the hillside (land) and not the trail, as trail "slope" is called the grade.

Slope, Percent Number of feet rise (vertical) divided by feet of run (horizontal) times 100 to get percent slope; example: 15 feet of rise over 100 feet of run is a 15 percent slope.

Slough Ingress, egress, or backflow from a creek or river. Usually areas full of soft, deep mud.

Snag Any standing dead, partially dead, or defective (cull) tree at least 10 inches in diameter at breast height and at least 6 feet tall.

Sojourn Continuing or remaining in a place. A temporary stay.

Sojourner One who stays as a temporary resident.

Space blanket An ultra light, windproof and water-proof emergency blanket made of aluminized mylar that is reflective silver on one side.

Species A unit of classification of plants and animals consisting of the largest and most inclusive array or sexually reproducing and cross-fertilizing individuals that share a common gene pool.

Species, Invasive or Exotic Non-native plant or animal species that invades an area and alters the natural mix of species by aggressively out-competing native species.

Species, Sensitive Any plant or animal species for which population viability is a concern as evidenced by significant current or predicted downward trends in population numbers or density, or habitat capability that would reduce a species' existing distribution.

Species, Threatened or Endangered Any plant or animal species that is in danger of extinction throughout all or a significant portion of its range, and has been officially listed as endangered by the Secretary of Interior or Commerce under the provisions of the Endangered Species Act. A final rule for the listing has been published in the Federal Register.

Spillway A constructed passage for surplus water to run over or around a reservoir.

Spring (Seep, Seepage) A saturated zone at or near the ground surface where voids in the rock or soil are filled with water at greater that atmospheric pressure. A seep is a small spring.

Stand A community of trees possessing sufficient uniformity in composition, age arrangement, and condition as to be distinguishable from trees in adjoining areas.

State Land Lands administered by any one of several state agencies.

State Parks Parks and recreation areas owned and administered by the state in which they are located.

Steward The person taking responsibility for the wellbeing of land and water resources and doing something to restore or protect that wellbeing.

Stewardship Taking responsibility for the wellbeing of land and water resources and doing something to restore or protect that wellbeing. It usually involves cooperation among people with different interests and sharing of decision-making. It is generally voluntary. It is oriented towards assessment, protection, and rehabilitation of trails and greenways as well as sustainable use of renewable resources.

Stile A ramp, step, or set of steps for hikers to pass over a fence or wall without allowing livestock to escape.

Stream Small body of running water moving in a natural channel or bed.

Stream, Ephemeral A temporary or short-lived water flow only in direct response to a heavy rain. Most of the year it's a dry bed.

Stream, Intermittent Channels that naturally carry water part of the year and are dry the other part.

Stream, Perennial Stream channels that carry water year round.

Stream, Seasonal Channels that naturally carry water part of the year, typically during the winter and spring months, and are dry the other part.

Stream Bank The side slopes of an active channel between which the streamflow is normally confined.

Stream Crossing A trail crossing a body of running water at grade without the use of a developed structure or bridge.

Streambed The unvegetated portion of a channel boundary below the baseflow water level. The channel through which a natural stream of water runs or used to run, as a dry streambed.

Street Any public thoroughfare (street, avenue, boulevard, or park) or space more than 20 ft wide which has been dedicated or deeded to the public for public use.

Stuff Sack A water-repellant or waterproof bag with a drawstring, used for compact storage of gear.

Subalpine A terrestrial community that generally is found in harsher environments than the montane terrestrial community. Subalpine communities are generally colder than montane and support a unique clustering of wildlife species.

Summit: The highest point (top) of a mountain.

Summit, False You think you're at the top, but you're not. Keep climbing.

Suspension Bridge A bridge that has its treadway suspended from two or more cables securely anchored at the ends.

Sustainable (Sustainability) Community use of natural resources in a way that does not jeopardize the ability of future generations to live and prosper.

Swamp Low lying land saturated with moisture and overgrown with vegetation but not covered with water.

Switchback A sustainable sharp turn on a hillside (usually on a slope of more than 15%) to reverse the direction of travel and to gain elevation. The landing is the turning portion of the switchback. The approaches are the trail sections upgrade and downgrade from the landing.

Sylvan Of, found, or living in the woods or forest.

Tableland High flatland or plateau.

Take a hike Literally "Leave!" Recent use is less negative and imperative and can even be positive and encouraging.

Talus (Talus Slope) Large rock debris on a slope or at the base of a hill or cliff. The rocks are larger and have sharper edges than those found on scree slopes.

Tarn A small mountain lake or pond created by glacial movement.

Technical A section along a trail that is difficult to navigate; used by mountain bikers to describe challenging sections of trail.

Ten Essentials A list of "must pack" items first circulated in the 1930s by The Mountaineers, an outings club in Seattle, and now a kind of gospel among hikers. Traditional essentials include map, compass, water, extra food, extra clothing, first-aid kit, pocket knife, sun protection, flashlight, matches/fire-starter.

Ten Percent Rule Laying out a trail so that the over-all grade is under 10 percent with maximum not to exceed 15 percent.

Ten Percent Average Guideline Generally, an average trail grade of 10 percent or less is most sustainable. This does not mean that all trail grades must be kept under 10 percent. Many trails will have short sections steeper than 10 percent, and some unique situations will allow average trail grades of more than 10 percent.

Tent Site(s) A designated flat, dry spot where a tent may be pitched. Site may have a central fire pit and pit toilet.

Terminus Either the beginning or end of a trail.

Threatened Species Species of flora or fauna likely to become endangered within the foreseeable future.

Three-Hour Tour A short hike that looks all too easy at the trailhead until unforeseen events makes it an all-day affair.

Thru-Hiker Someone who attempts to cover a long trail, such as the Appalachian Trail, in one continuous trek.

Tide table A table giving daily predictions, usually a year in advance, of the times and heights of the tide for a number of reference stations.

Timber Line (Tree Line) The farthest limit, either in altitude on a mountain, or the farthest north in the northern hemisphere, in which trees are able to grow. Beyond this line, the environment is too harsh for trees to survive.

Topographic (Topo, USGS Topographic, Contour) Map Maps that indicate built and natural features (buildings, roads, ravines, rivers, etc.) as well as elevation changes and land cover. United States Geological Survey maps are available from many government offices, outdoor shops, and map stores; or from digitized versions on the Internet.

Topographic Of or having to do with topography or the physical features of a place.

Topography The elevation and slope of the land as it exists or is proposed. It is represented on drawings by lines connecting points at the same elevation. Typically illustrated by dashed lines for existing topography and solid lines for proposed.

Toponym A place name.

Torrent A turbulent, swift-flowing stream. A heavy downpour, a deluge.

Touron Park rangers contrived the word (a combination of tourist and moron) to describe a person who behaves stupidly in the great outdoors.

Track Mark left by something that has passed along; footprint or wheel rut.

Trail A designated route on land or water with public access for recreation or transportation purposes such as walking, jogging, hiking, bicycling, horseback riding, mountain biking, canoeing and kayaking.

Trail, Access Any trail that connects the main trail to a town, road, or another trail or trail system.

Trail, Backcountry A primitive trail in an area where there are no maintained roads or permanent buildings.

Trail, Blaze This expression was first used literally in the 18th century for the practice of marking a forest trail by making blazes, that is, marking trees with notches or chips in the bark.

Trail, Braided (Braiding) The process or name of undesirable multiple parallel paths created by users.

Trail, Connecting or Side Name give to trails providing additional points of access to national recreation, scenic, or historic trails per the National Trails System Act.

Trail, Contour A trail constructed or exists such that it follows a contour, with its elevation remaining constant.

Trail, Designated Specific trails identified by the land management agency where some type of use (motorized or nonmotorized) is appropriate and allowed either seasonally or yearlong and which have been inventoried and mapped and are appropriately signed on the ground.

Trail, Destination A trail that connects two distinct points (A to B) rather than returning the user to the original beginning point.

Trail, Directional Use (One-way) A trail laid out in such a way as to encourage users to travel in one direction.

Trail, Doubletrack A trail that allows for two users to travel side by side, or to pass without one user having to yield the trail. Doubletrack trails are often old forest or fire roads.

Trail, Extended Trails more than 100 miles in length (as defined in the National Trails System Act).

Trail, Feeder A trail designed to connect local facilities, neighborhoods, campgrounds, etc. to a main trail.

Trail, Flat A trail built across level terrain. The terrain is without a pronounced cross slope.

Trail, Frontcountry Less emphasis is put on minimizing contact with signs of the civilized world.

The main objective is to provide enjoyable trail experiences within the vicinity of developed areas by utilizing the scenic and interpretative features of semi-urban, rural, and natural environments.

Trail, Greenway (Urban Trail) A trail established along a natural corridor, such as a river, stream, ridgeline, rail trail, canal, or other route for conservation, recreation, or alternative transportation purposes. Greenway Trails can connect parks, nature preserves, cultural facilities, and historic sites with business and residential areas.

Trail, Hiker-Biker An urban paved trail designed for use by pedestrians and bicyclists.

Trail, Hiking Moderate to long distance trail with the primary function of providing long-distance walking experiences (usually two miles or more).

Trail, Interpretive (Nature Trail) Short to moderate length trail (1/2 to 1 mile) with primary function of providing an opportunity to walk or hike and study interesting or unusual plants or natural features at user's pleasure. The ideal nature trail has a story to tell. It unifies the various features or elements along the trail into a related theme.

Trail, Long Distance In general a trail best characterized by length (more than 50 miles), linearity (follows a linear feature), and diversity (geographic and political).

Trail, Loop(ed) Trail or trail systems designed so that the routes are closed circuits connecting a number of points of interest, giving users the option of not traveling the same section of trail more than once on a trip.

Trail, Multiple-Use (Multi-Use, Diversified Use, Shared Use) A trail that permits more than one user group at a time (equestrian, hiker, mountain bicyclist, etc.).

Trail, Out-and-Back A one-way trail on which you travel to a destination then backtrack to the trailhead.

Trail, Pack A trail used by recreational stock; usually extended trails used by pack strings for overnight trips.

Trail, Primary Continuous through route that originates at a trailhead. Primarily for directing users through an area while promoting a certain type of experience.

Trail, Recreation A trail that is designed to provide a recreational experience.

Trail, Regional An extended or longer trail that may cross one or more land management agency jurisdictions and connects diverse trail systems.

Trail, Secondary Short trail used to connect primary trails or branches of primary trails. They encourage movement between two primary trails or facilitate dispersal of use through secondary branching.

Trail, Side Dead-end trail that accesses features near the main trail.

Trail, Single-Track A trail so narrow that users must generally travel in a single file.

Trail, Single-Use One that is designed and constructed for only one intended use (i.e. hiking only).

Trail, Soft Surface An unsurfaced natural trail or a trail surfaced with compacted earth, crusher fines, bark, or gravel.

Trail, Spur A trail that leads from primary, secondary, or spine trails to points of user interests such as overlooks, campsites, etc.

Trail, Stacked Loop Trail or trail systems designed with many loops "stacked" on each other, giving users the option of not traveling the same section of trail more than once on a trip.

Trail, Stock A route/trail used by commercial stock.

Trail, Undesignated (Social, Wildcat, Way, Informal, User or Visitor Created) Any unofficial trails that develop informally from use and are not designated or maintained by an agency; often found cutting switchbacks or between adjacent trails, campsites, or other sites of interest. Undesignated trails can be dangerous, eroded, and unsustainable.

Trail Angel(s) Name given to anyone who goes out of their way to help out a trail user by offering food, shelter, or a ride into town out of the goodness of their hearts rather than for profit or gain.

Trail Community Includes those with an interest in, or relationship to a particular trail (long distance or system): volunteers, landowners, government agency personnel, and the officials and citizens of local communities through which the trail passes or trail system is located. For example, there is the Appalachian Trail community.

Trail Design Designing and layout of trails requires special training, knowledge, experience, and skill. When designing trails, many different factors are taken into account including hydrology, topography, soils, flora, fauna, management objectives, user expectations and characteristics, and trail design standards. The designer will utilize data collected from area site analysis, environmental assessments, public meetings, and area trail and management plans.

Trail Magic The special unexpected pleasures that happen and the generosity that trail users experience while on a trail trip.

Trail Name A chosen or given nickname a trail user adopts while on an extended trail trip to identify themselves when making register entries, often based on personality, lifestyle, or traveling style.

Trail Runner(s) People who find pleasure running on trails instead of asphalt.

Trail System(s) A collection of individual trails that may or may not be connected to one another, whereby each retains its distinctiveness, and yet belongs to the system by association with a federal, state, local, or bioregional context.

Trailbed The finished surface on which base course or surfacing may be constructed. For trails without surfacing, the trailbed is the tread.

Trailblazer One who blazes a trail. An innovative leader or pioneer in a field.

Trailbuilder(s) Those that build trails.

Trailhead Beginning of a trail, the point at which a path starts. An area with access to hiking, biking or horseback riding where parking is permitted and often accompanied by various public facilities, such, toilets, water, directional and informational signs, and a trail use register.

Trample (Trampling) To tread heavily so as to bruise, crush, or injure; refers to the process of vegetation being destroyed by trail users.

Traverse To cross a slope horizontally going gradually up and across in lieu of the more direct up-and-over (up the fall line) approach.

Tread (Treadway) The surface portion of a trail upon which users travel. Common tread surfaces are native material, gravel, soil cement, asphalt, concrete, or shredded recycled tires.

Tread Lightly! Educational program designed to instill outdoor ethics of responsible behavior when participating in outdoor activities.

Tree Any woody plant that normally grows to a mature height greater than 20 feet and has a diameter of four inches or more at a point four feet above the ground.

Tree Line (Timber Line) The farthest limit, either in altitude on a mountain, or the farthest north in the northern hemisphere, in which trees are able to grow. Beyond this line, the environment is too harsh for trees to survive.

Trek To hike a long way. Trekkers are long-distance hikers.

Trekking Pole(s) Telescoping hiking poles used in pairs. Each pole, when planted, reduces weight on the legs and back thereby reducing fatigue, increasing speed, and providing stability when hiking with or without a backpack.

Triangulation System of equating compass and maps to a known landmark.

Tributary A river or stream feeding into a larger waterway or lake.

Triple Crown Trails The Appalachian Trail (2,167 miles long), the Pacific Crest Trail (2,650 miles), and the Continental Divide Trail (approximately 3100 miles) are known as the "Triple Crown" of long-distance trails.

True North The direction toward the geographic North Pole. Most maps are oriented to True North.

Tumpline A strap slung over the forehead, to anchor a backpack.

Turn Where a trail changes course or direction.

Turnout A place where the trail is widened to permit trail traffic traveling in opposite directions to pass.

Turtling To fall backwards onto one's backpack at an angle that makes it exceedingly difficult to right oneself. Always funny when it happens to someone else.

Ultralighter (Ultralight Backpacker) A backpacker who carries the absolute minimum.

Underpass An underground tunnel or passage enabling trail users to cross under a road or railway.

Understory All forest vegetation growing under the canopy or upper layers of forest vegetation.

Upland Land at a higher elevation than the alluvial plain or low stream terrace; all lands outside the riparian-wetland and aquatic zones.

Urban Places within boundaries set by state and local officials having a population of 5,000 or more.

Urban Interface An area characterized by an intermingling of residential private land with federal lands.

User Fee Any charge for use of services, facilities, trails, or areas. Examples include trail use fees, entrance fees, parking fees, shelter fees, or voluntary donations.

Valley A long, narrow land area lying between two areas of higher elevation, often containing a stream.

Vegetation Plant life; growing plants.

Vegetation, Native Indigenous species that are normally found as part of a particular ecosystem; a species that was present in a defined area prior to European settlement.

Viewpoint A place affording a view of something. Also, a position of observation.

Viewshed The landscape that can be directly seen under favorable atmospheric conditions from a viewpoint or along a trail corridor.

Visitor-Day, Recreation (RVD) 12 hours of recreation at a given site. One recreation visitor-day can be one person for 12 hours, 2 people for 6 hours, 12 people for 1 hour and so on. Used by agencies to count visits to developed sites, trails, and backcountry.

Visitors Total number of people that visit an area during some unit of time, usually a year. Used by agencies to count visits to developed sites, trails, and backcountry.

Vista A distant view or prospect, especially one seen through an opening, as between rows of trees.

Vitamin I Ibuprofen: a pain-reliever often used by hikers, considered essential during the first week of a long-distance hike.

Volunteer Person who works on a trail or for a trail club without pay.

Walk To move along on foot; to advance by steps. To go on foot for exercise or pleasure To pass on foot or as if on foot through, along, over, or upon. To cause (an animal or human) to go at a walk. To accompany on foot.

Walk-up A summit that can be reached without technical climbing skills. Most summits favored by hikers are walk-ups, even such significant peaks as Mt. Whitney, highest peak in the continental U.S.

Wash Removal or erosion of soil by the action of moving water. The dry bed of a stream, particularly a watercourse associated with arid environments and characterized by large, high-energy discharges with high bed-material load transport.

Washout Erosion of a relatively soft surface, such as a trail, by a sudden gush of water, as from a downpour or floods. A channel produced by such erosion.

Water filter A portable device for removing contaminants (particularly giardia) from drinking waters.

Waterbar A drainage structure (for turning water) composed of an outsloped segment of tread leading to a barrier (log, stone, or timber) placed at a 45 degree angle to the trail.

Waterfall Sudden, near vertical descent of water from a height as it flows over rock or a steep embankment.

Watershed (Drainage Basin, Catchment Basin)
A region or area bounded peripherally by a water parting formation (i.e. ridge, hill, mountain range) and draining ultimately to a particular watercourse or body of water.

Waterway(s) The volume of water distinguishes waterways. Rivers have the greatest volume, followed by streams, creeks, and brooks.

Waypoint A point between major points on a route, as along a track.

Weathering The physical and chemical disintegration and decomposition of rocks and minerals.

Weed A plant considered undesirable, unattractive, or troublesome, usually introduced and growing without intentional cultivation.

Wetland(s) Lowland areas, such as a marshes or bogs that are saturated with water, creating unique habitat for plants and wildlife.

White-out Extremely heavy snow conditions with near-zero visibility. May also refer to thick fog or low-hanging clouds or dust that produce the same effect.

Width, Tread The width of the portion of the trail used for travel.

Wilderness Undeveloped land and associated

water resources retaining their primeval character and influence.

Wilderness Act of 1964 Act of Congress that established federal Wilderness Areas. As defined, Wilderness Areas are undeveloped federal lands without permanent improvements or human habitation that are protected and managed so as to preserve natural conditions. The Act prohibits the use of mechanized vehicles and construction in Wilderness Areas.

Wilderness Area Uninhabited and undeveloped federal land to which Congress has granted special status and protection under authority of the Wilderness Act of 1964. Allows foot and horse traffic only; no mountain bikes, OHV use, hang gliders, or other "machines."

Wildland(s) Ecologically healthy lands that are in their original natural state.

Wildlife Any undomesticated animal species living in its natural habitat including birds (raptors, songbirds, upland game birds), mammals (furbearers, big game, nongame mammals), reptiles, amphibians, and fish.

Windchill The cooling effect that results from wind and cold; especially dramatic if wearing wet clothes.

Windfall (Wildthrow, Downfall) Anything (trees, limbs, brush, etc.) blown down on the trail by the wind.

Yield Being prepared to yield the trail to another user by slowing down, preparing to stop, establishing communication, and passing safely.

Yo-Yo(ing) Turning around after completing a long-distance trail trip and returning to the start making it a round-trip.

Yo-yoer A thru-hiker who reaches trail's end only to run around and hike back to the beginning.

Yogi(ing) Trail users "yogi" when they entice a non-trail user out of something they need or want without actually asking for it. Named after Yogi the Bear from cartoon fame because of his habit of making off with people's picnic baskets.

Zero-Mile Mark The point at which a measured trail starts.

Zipline Rigging system with a taut, stationary wire rope highline for moving loads on a movable pulley.

English English for Hikers

American English and the English spoken by hikers in England, Ireland, Scotland and Wales are not exactly the same language. Here are some words and terms used by hikers in the British Isles and beyond:

Aye Yes (Scotland, northern England)
Beck Stream
Ben Mountain (Scotland)
Biscuit Cookie
Brae Hill (Scotland)
Burn Stream (Scotland)
Downs Rolling, grassy hills
Drove Road Ancient route used to bring livestock to market
Glen Valley (Scotland)

Glyn Valley (Wales)

Jumper Sweater

Kissing Gate Swinging gate that allows passage of hikers (but not animals)

Ladder Stile Over walls and fences via two ladders, back to back

Moor High, open, treeless area

Ordnance Survey (OS) The British mapping agency

Pen Peak (Wales)

Pike Peak (northern England)

Ramble A short to medium length hike

Sack Backpack

Squeeze Gate Narrow gap in wall allows people, not animals, through

Tarn Small mountain lake

Twitchers Avid bird-watchers

Way A long distance trail

Hike. Contemplate what makes you happy and what makes you happier still. Follow a trail or blaze a new one. **Hike.** Think about what you can do to expand your life and someone else's. **Hike.** Slow down. Gear up. **Hike.** Connect with friends. Re-connect with nature.

Hike. Shed stress. Feel blessed. Hike to remember. Hike to forget. Hike for recovery. Hike for discovery. **Hike.** Enjoy the beauty of providence. **Hike.** Share the way, The Hiker's Way, on the long and winding trail we call life.

About the Author

JOHN MCKINNEY

www.TheTrailmaster.com

JOHN MCKINNEY is the author of 25 books about hiking, parklands and nature, including *The Hiker's Way: Hike Smart, Live Well, Go Green* and *A Walk Along Land's End, Dispatches from the Edge of California* on a 1,600-mile hike from Mexico to Oregon.

McKinney has written more than a thousand articles about hiking plus numerous trail guidebooks including such popular favorites as *Southern California, A Day Hiker's Guide* and *Day Hiker's Guide to California's State Parks*. His books for children include *Let's go Geocaching* and *Let's go Hiking*.

For 18 years, McKinney, a.k.a. The Trailmaster,

wrote a weekly hiking column for the *Los Angeles Times.* A passionate advocate for hiking and our need to reconnect with nature, McKinney shares his expertise on radio and TV, and as a public speaker.

HIKE ON.

www.TheTrailmaster.com